Model Boat Building

The Spritsail Skiff

Schiffer Publishing Ltd

77 Lower Valley Road, Atglen, PA 19310

Steve Rogers &
Patricia Staby-Rogers

Published by Schiffer Publishing, Ltd.
77 Lower Valley Road
Atglen, PA 19310
Please write for a free catalog.
This book may be purchased from the publisher.
Please include $2.95 postage.
Try your bookstore first.

We are interested in hearing from authors
with book ideas on related subjects.

CONTENTS

Copyright © 1993 by Steve Rogers and Patricia Staby-Rogers.
Library of Congress Catalog Number: 93-85082.

Printed in the United States of America.
ISBN: 0-88740-534-7

Introduction

There is a road that goes from Princess Anne, Maryland on Route 13 West to Deal's Island. As you travel you pass small farm houses, fields, and stands of yellow pine. In the winter the landscape is quiet, washed in rusts, brown, and tan accented by the dark green of the pines. Suddenly you emerge from a short stretch of woods and the broad expanse of the marsh opens up in front of you. Extending all the way to the horizon, there seems to be no end of it. It's criss-crossed by a myriad of ditches, creeks, and rivers before it merges with the Chesapeake Bay. As desolate and vast as this landscape seems, people live here. They make their living by harvesting the various fisheries of the bay crabs, oysters, clams, and fish. The people were here before the roads, before the bridge. They got around in the boats that they designed and built by themselves.

These small craft are not the yachts of the idle rich but the hard-driven boats of the watermen. Sometimes their beauty is simply in a fine line. More often it is in the careful, functional design the watermen incorporate in their construction.

This book is about building a model of one of the many truly ingenious and unique craft that developed in this environment. This particular boat is called a North Carolina Spritsail Skiff and was primarily used in the vast inland bays of the outer banks of North Carolina. There was a significant exchange of design ideas between the Chesapeake Bay and the outer banks but ultimately each area developed its own particular designs to match its environment.

The North Carolina Spritsail is a shallow draft sailing craft, good for getting around Pamlico Sound. The Maritime Museum in Beaufort, North Carolina has a very good example of this boat and I've used the plans drawn by Mike Alford extensively to develop this model. We'll build this boat in one inch scale (meaning one inch equals one foot). This is an easy scale to work in and will make a nice size for the model. We will be building it in much the same way as the actual boat was built.

This particular boat has a shallow vee bottom and a centerboard. The forward part of the bottom is not planked, but shaped from solid chunks of wood fastened together. Heavy thwarts support the centerboard case fore and aft, and the Spritsail rig with the optional top sail allows sailing in a broad range of wind conditions. It's a large boat with serious capacity to haul or work over the expanses of the coastal bays.

I advise you to read through this book once before you begin making the model. When I work I build some components while others dry, so occasionally the sequence of steps may be confusing. Some steps in the construction are simply repetitions and are therefore not shown in great detail. In any case, the more clearly you understand the process, the easier the building will be.

I've also made some minor changes in dimensions and details for reasons of simplification, but this in no way affects the authenticity of the final result. I should also add that the process of fitting the bottom frames is not a speed test. Take your time and use your sanding block to carefully achieve a close fit. It helps to visualize the shape that the finished piece must be. Remember, the saw gets you close and the sanding block makes the fit. Make a point of studying the detail drawings and relating them to the jig.

The Materials

The following is a list of the supplies you will need:

2—1″ x 4″ x 6′ clear pine boards
20-gauge ½″ brads
½″ sequin pins
20-gauge ½″ nails
Aliphatic resin glue (yellow woodworking glue)
24-gauge galvanized wire
1″ 18-gauge brads
Round toothpicks
Rigging line (1 hank medium)
1/32″ brass rod (1—12″ length)

gray primer (spray can)
Latex paint: ceiling white, bottom paint, light green trim
Stain
Acrylic colors; burnt umber, ivory black, burnt sienna, yellow orange Azo
Drafting ink
½ yard unbleached cotton muslin (don't skimp; buy the best grade available; permanent press is fine)
White or off-white thread
Tan or medium brown thread

Detailed Drawings

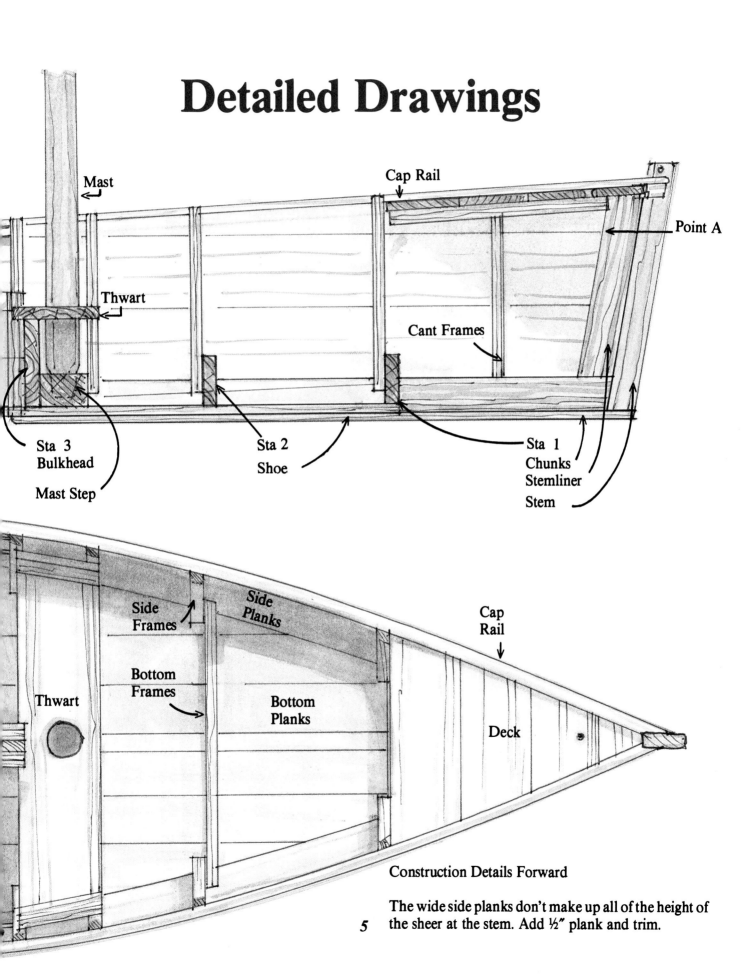

Mast

Cap Rail

Point A

Thwart

Cant Frames

Sta 3
Bulkhead

Mast Step

Sta 2
Shoe

Sta 1
Chunks
Stemliner
Stem

Side
Frames

Side
Planks

Bottom
Frames

Bottom
Planks

Thwart

Cap
Rail

Deck

Construction Details Forward

The wide side planks don't make up all of the height of
the sheer at the stem. Add ½″ plank and trim.

5

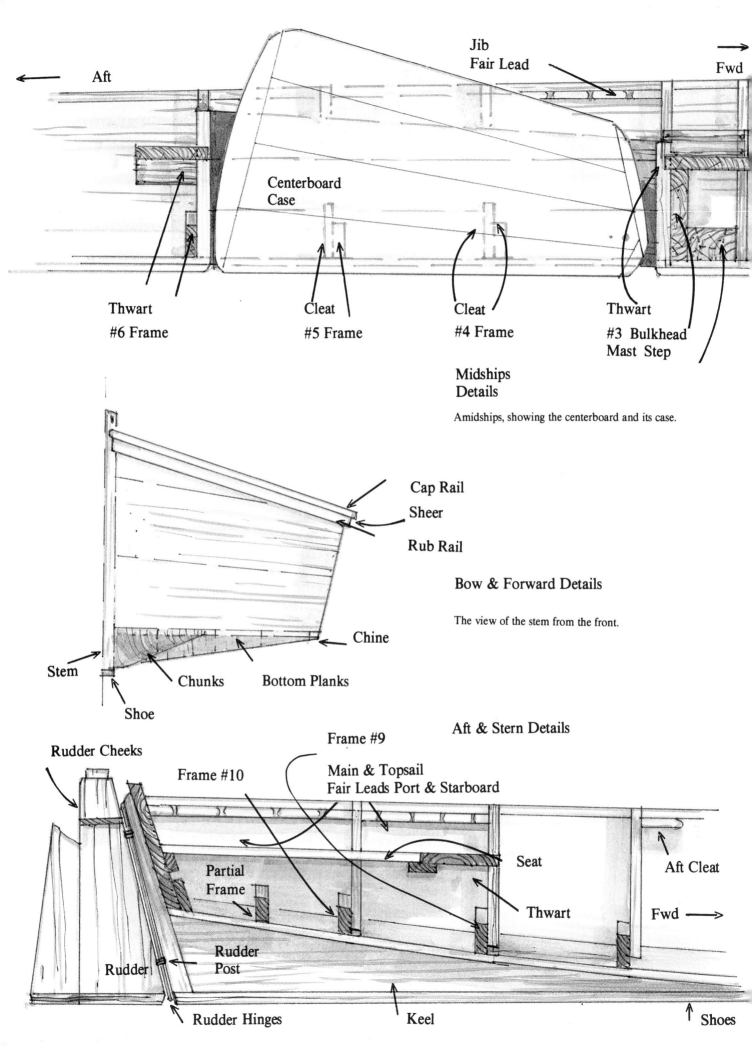

Aft ←

Jib
Fair Lead

Fwd →

Centerboard
Case

Thwart
#6 Frame

Cleat
#5 Frame

Cleat
#4 Frame

Thwart
#3 Bulkhead
Mast Step

Midships
Details

Amidships, showing the centerboard and its case.

Cap Rail

Sheer

Rub Rail

Bow & Forward Details

The view of the stem from the front.

Chine

Stem

Chunks   Bottom Planks

Shoe

Aft & Stern Details

Frame #9

Rudder Cheeks

Frame #10

Main & Topsail
Fair Leads Port & Starboard

Seat

Aft Cleat

Partial
Frame

Thwart

Fwd →

Rudder

Rudder
Post

Rudder Hinges   Keel

Shoes

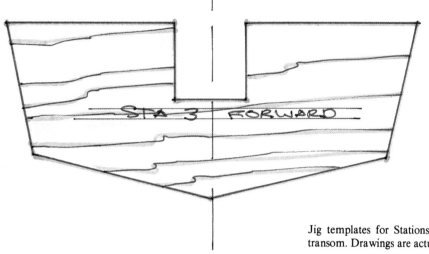

STA 3 FORWARD

The Jig

Jig templates for Stations 3 (forward), Station 6 (aft face) and the transom. Drawings are actual size.

JIG TEMPLATE

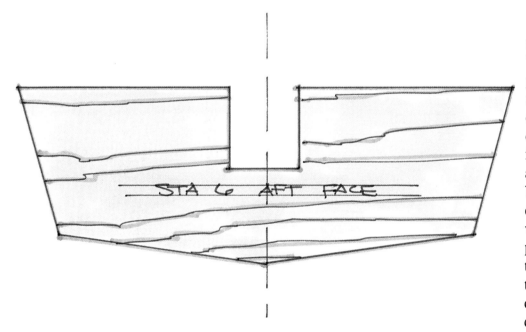

STA 6 AFT FACE

We're going to build this model on a prefabricated jig. The jig will keep the hull in perfect alignment and maintain the correct shape during construction. It will designate the location of the frames, the forward chunks, and the transom while you build, and will hold these components securely in place while you apply the bottom planking. After you remove the planked hull from the jig, the location of the remaining components such as the centerboard case, the thwarts, and the mast step will be self-evident.

Allow for slight bevel on forward face of transom

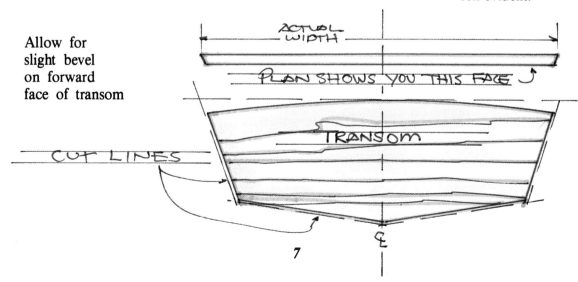

ACTUAL WIDTH

PLAN SHOWS YOU THIS FACE

TRANSOM

CUT LINES

7

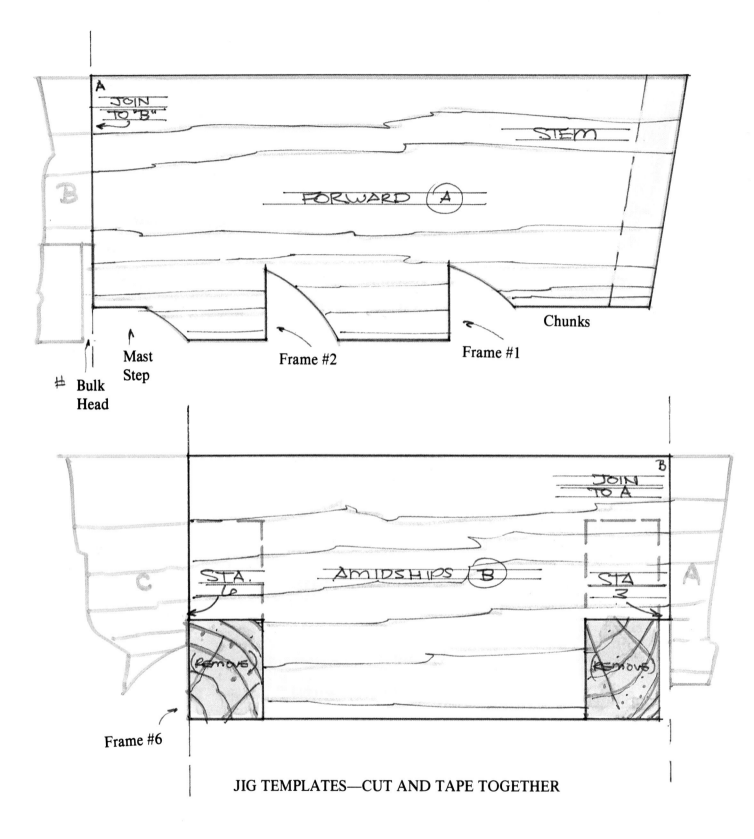

A

JOIN
TO "B"

STEM

FORWARD (A)

Chunks

Mast
Step

Frame #2

Frame #1

⌗ Bulk
Head

B

JOIN
TO A

STA. 6

AMIDSHIPS (B)

STA 3

C

(remove)

(remove)

A

Frame #6

JIG TEMPLATES—CUT AND TAPE TOGETHER

The three patterns, forward (A), amidships (B), and aft (C), need to be cut
and taped together. The transom pad is tacked onto the end. Everything is
drawn actual size.

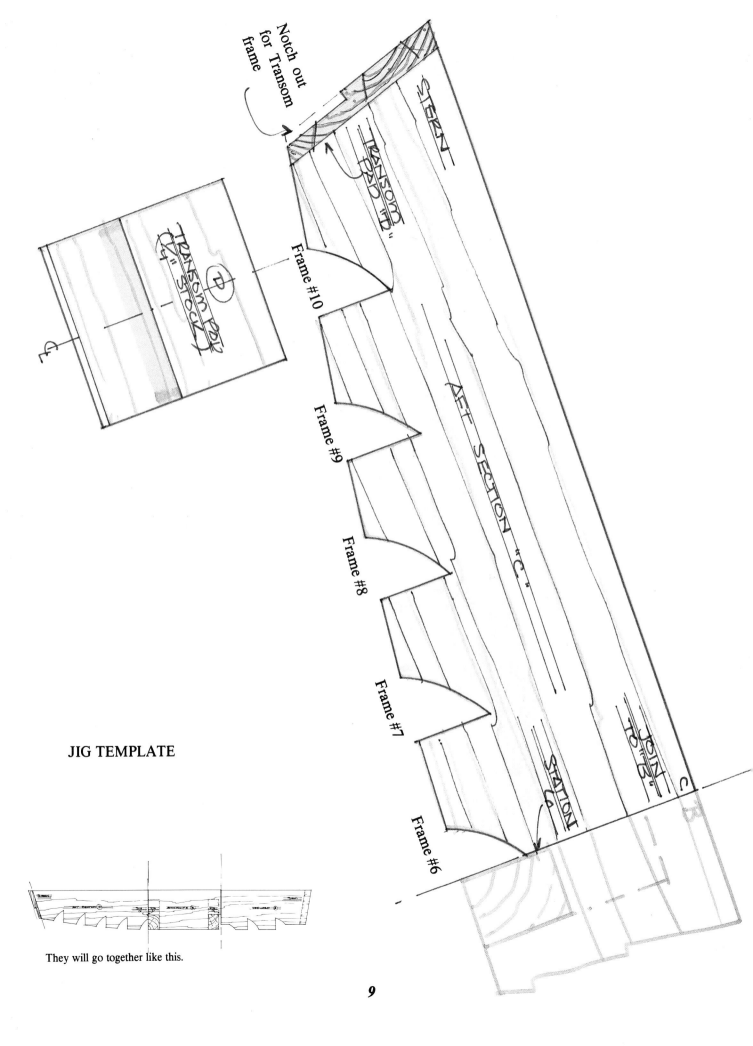

Notch out
for Transom
frame

TRANSOM PD12
(4" STOCK)

TRANSOM
PAD "D"

STERN

Frame #10

Frame #9

Frame #8

AFT SECTION "C"

Frame #7

Frame #6

STATION 6

JOIN
TO "B"

C B

JIG TEMPLATE

They will go together like this.

9

This is a picture of the jig in its early stages of development. I've provided templates for you to use but here I'm locating all of the structural components of the hull.

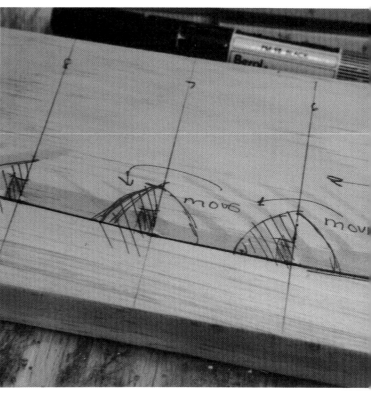

Here we establish frame stations and access to them on the jig.

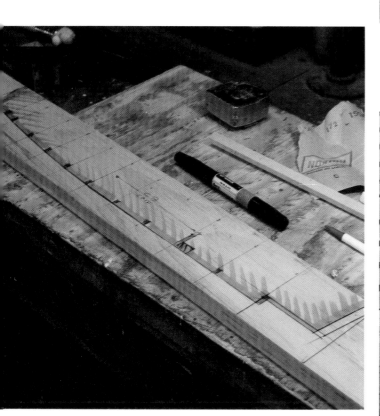

The yellow area is the actual size of the jig.

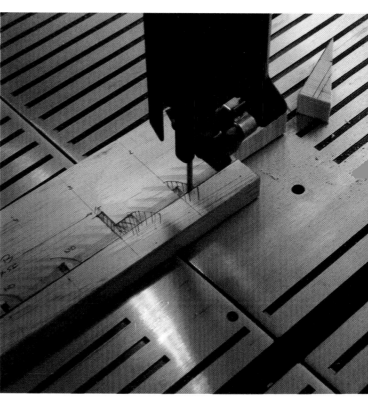

Saw out the longitudinal jig on a band saw.

Trace and cut out the cross-section portions of the jig.

Shave a taper on the front part of the jig in order to make room for the side planks.

Glue and assemble the jig.

The assembled jig.

This was an afterthought on my part. The pad shown on the end (an appropriate amount of jig was cut away) will help hold the transom at a right angle to the center line.

Building the Boat

This is a 1″ x 4″ x 6′ board.

Mark, using a square.

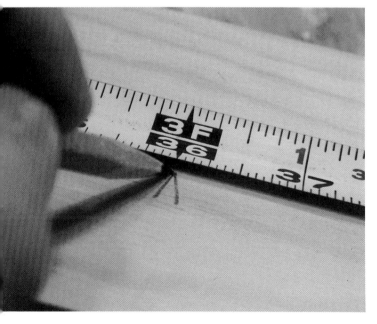

Divide the board in half.

Cut in half.

Dry fit with the annual rings in opposition.

Here's our glued-up board ready to saw.

Apply glue to one face of the boards.

This is the blade I use to saw my stock.

Clamp together and set aside to dry.

Rip a 3/32" thick piece from the board assembly and inspect it for uniformity and flaws. When you're satisfied, saw several pieces for use as side planks, centerboard, and rudder stock.

This is a picture of the jig and some of the stock I cut on the table saw from the other 1″ x 4″. Each piece is 36″ long and the sizes are as follows:

⅛″ x ⅛″ x 36″ 2 pieces

⅛″ x ¼″ x 36″ 2 pieces

⅛″ x ½″ x 36″ 4 pieces

⅛″ x ¾″ x 36″ 4 pieces

3/32″ x ½″ x 36″ 16 pieces

3/32″ x ¾″ x 36″ 4 pieces

3/32″ x ¼″ x 36″ 6 pieces

7/16″ x ½″ x 36″ 1 piece

7/16″ x 7/16″ x 36″ 4 pieces

9/16″ x 9/16″ x 36″ 2 pieces

3/32″ x 3/32″ x 36″ 2 pieces

1/16″ x ⅛″ x 24″ 2 pieces

   Some of the stock is slightly oversized but subsequent sanding and planing will correct that. **Extra margins for error is always good to have.**

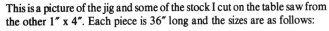

Cut side frames from ⅛″ x ½″ stock. Taper them.

This is a step you'll be able to skip because I've provided a template of the expanded transom assembly. On a plan, the transom is never the shape it appears because the view on the ship's lines is perpendicular. The transom is angled so it appears to have less height than it actually does. The lines always include the thickness of the bottom and side planks so the actual transom itself is smaller than the lines indicate. Also, the transom is a three dimensional assembly and is beveled so that the forward face that you can't see is wider than the face you're looking at. As a result, extra width is necessary to achieve the bevel.

Trace and cut out the transom.

Glue and clamp the transom to the side frames.

For strength, I fit some additional framing to the bottom edge of the transoms. Use ⅛″ x ½″ stock. Trim.

Plane and sand the stem liner from the 7/16″ x ½″ stock. Make the forward face ⅛″ wide and the aft face ½″.

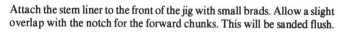

Attach the stem liner to the front of the jig with small brads. Allow a slight overlap with the notch for the forward chunks. This will be sanded flush.

I notched the transom pad of the template to allow for the additional framing.

Nail the transom to the pad with ½″ nails.

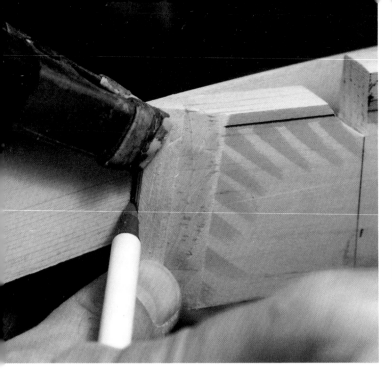

With your jig in a vise, bend your 1½″ wide planks around and clamp. Mark for cutting. As you fasten the side planks to the jig, make sure the bottom edge meets the points established by the jig at the stem liner, station 3 and station 6. A slight mismatch at the transom is normal. Don't try to make it fit at the transom by force because you'll distort the hull shape amidships. Make certain your sides lie flat on stations 3 and 6. This is the purpose of the jig.

Fasten with ½″ brads and glue at the stemliner and the transom (Note: the bottom edge of the plank may fall slightly above the transom but will be planed to shape.)

Fasten the side planks to stations 3 and 6.

Make your cut about 1/16″ past the mark you just made.

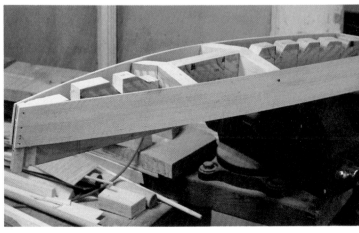

After you add the other side you can see the shape of the boat.

This is the first frame aft of the chunks. Use the ⅛″ x ¾″ stock. Mark the width and cut with a slight bevel and slight flare.

Remove, trim, re-install, glue and tack in place. All of the frames will be sanded at once, later.

Allow the frame to engage the sides by about a quarter of an inch. Mark on the back how high above the centerline the frame extends. Mark and cut along the line. This sets the depth of the frame.

Since the bottom deadrise is essentially consistent, this is a template I made to mark the bottom frames.

Re-install and mark the angle on the bottom from the center of the jig to the sides.

The second frame shape is derived the same way as the first. Once the width is determined on the jig, the bottom profile marked, the final shape is determined by marking the depth with a piece of ¼″ wide scrap.

Saw to shape.

When the glue is dry, mark the centerline and chine width on the piece.

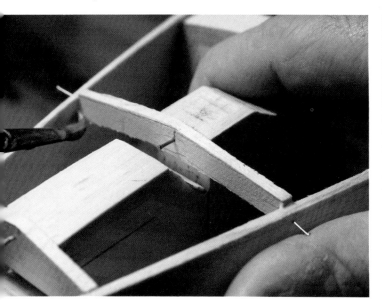

Glue and pin in place. Use ½" sequin pins to secure the side plank to the frame. Use ½" brads to fasten the frame to the jig.

Trace the bottom profile with your template.

Glue some ¾" x ⅛" stock and some ¼" x ⅛" stock together for a 1" wide piece for the station 3 bulkhead.

The bevel is minimal, but you can add a little flare when you cut.

Check the bottom angle against the station 3 jig.

Mark a centerline.

Cut on your lines and install. Don't worry if the frame extends above the chine slightly. This will be corrected when all the frames are sanded true. Don't forget to brush away any excess glue with a moist brush.

Trace a bottom profile.

Cut a 5″ piece of the 7/16″ x 1/2″ stock for the mast step.

Cut on your lines.

Mark the width, trim to fit.

Clean up any irregularity with a knife.

Glue to the station 3 bulkhead. Clean away excess glue.

It should look like this.

Moving back to the stem, sand the area where the sides and the stemliner come together forward of the first frame.

Glue together four 3″ long pieces of the 9/16″ x 9/16″ stock. Mark and cut a straight edge at one end.

Mark the shape of the chine.

Here's where we are.

Cut, allowing for a slight amount of excess.

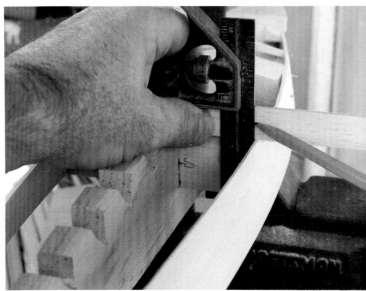

Move aft to station 6. Mark the width at the chine on a piece of ¾″ x ⅛″ stock.

Glue in place.

After you trace the frame bottom profile with your template, draw the top profile using the ¼″ scrap piece.

Round the intersection of the two sides.

Notch in limber holes.

Cut with a slight flare in the bevel.

The saw gets you close.

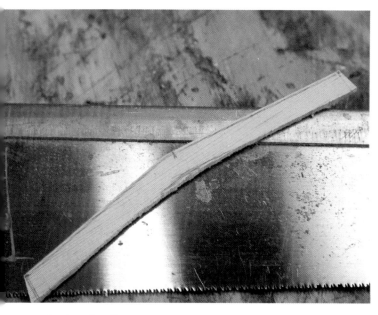

Ready to install.

The sanding block makes the fit.

Glue and fasten, allowing about 1/16″ above the chine line.

Drive in...

Install the rest of the frames, following the same procedure. Use the ½″ brads to secure the frame to the jig. Use glue and sequin pins to fasten the frame to the sides.

like so.

When dry, clip off the sequin pins close.

Carefully sand the entire bottom, keeping the sanding block on as many points as possible.

Clean up with 150 weight sanding paper.

Glue and pin, removing the excess glue with brush.

Dry fit a piece of ¼″ x 3/32″ stock for the keelson. It runs length-wise from the chunks to the transom.

Using a piece of ½″ x 3/32″ planking stock, fasten one end at the chunks and, allowing it to lie flat on the frames forward of station 6, bend it down to the transom. Don't force any deflection. Simply note the amount that the plank overlaps the keelson at the transom. Also note where this overlap begins amidships. This is called the garboard plank.

Mark the length.

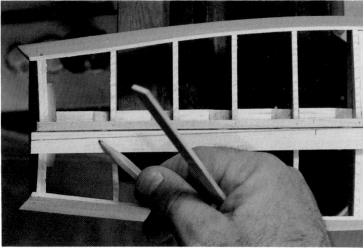

Draw a line between these two points.

Plane away the excess stock.

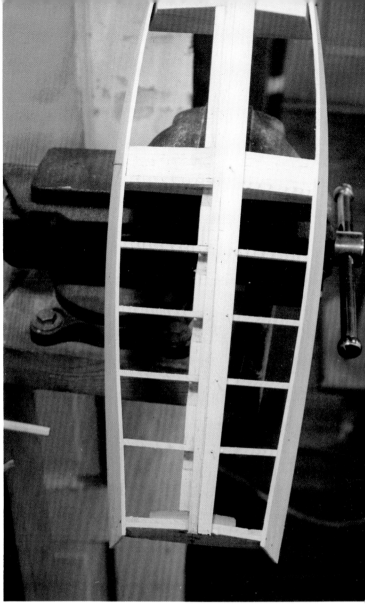

Glue and pin the garboard plank in place.

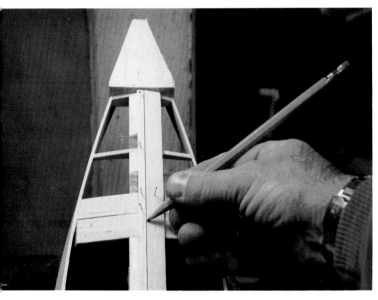

During the dry fitting stage, make note of the width of the gap between the plank and the keelson.

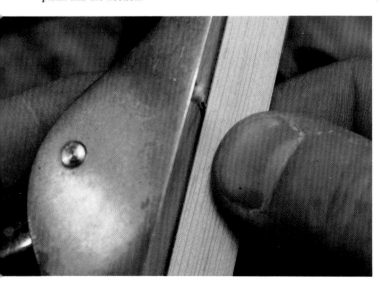

Duplicate that same gap between the sole of your plane and the plank. Carefully plane away until the gap disappears. This bevel will run the length of the plank.

Turn over and brush away any excess glue.

Repeat this procedure for the garboard plank on the opposite side. Then you can begin applying the bottom planks.

⅛″ x ½″ x 2″ Piece
Each end is divided into three equal parts and a diagonal is struck across the marks. Saw along the diagonal.

Making side frames.

Keep planking one side and then the other.

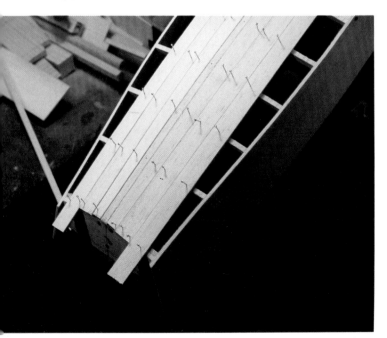

Continue planking until the bottom is completely covered. Glue and pin wherever the bottom contacts framing or the side plank. Brush out glue blobs. After the planking dries, leave the hull on the jig and trim away excess planking. Cut the planks that overlap the chine with either a saw or a knife, but leave a little excess. Use a sanding block to remove any remaining overlap until the bottom is flush with the sides.

Remove all the nails you've used to fasten the transom, the bottom frames and the stem liner to the jig (remove any other nails in the sides as well). Return the assembly to a vise and carefully (slowly) apply pressure, pulling all around the hull. Flex the hull as much as possible. It won't part from the jig without some resistance, but with patience you will suddenly feel it let go and separate.

26

All of the side frames are made the same way. I divide the ends of a 2″ long piece of ½″ x ⅛″ stock into three parts.

Sand a slight bevel (depending on the location in the boat) on the edge.

Cut, diagonally from one end, to the other, ending up with two equal, tapered pieces.

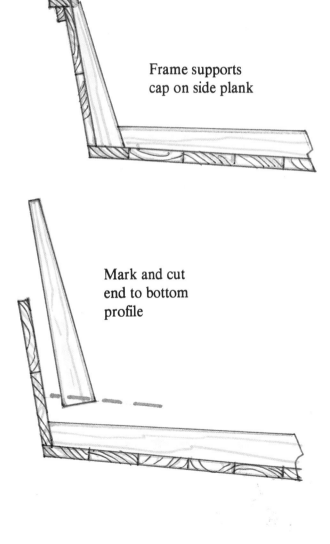

Frame supports cap on side plank

Mark and cut end to bottom profile

Cut a slight angle on the wide ends.

Fitting the side frame to the hull.

By trial and error, fit side frames, overlapping each of the bottom frames. The frame fits on the forward face of frames 6 through 10 and the aft face of frames 1 through 5. Use a sanding block to achieve a close fit.

At station 3 mark a point just under the top plank.

Install the first several side frames. Allow to dry and add a ½″ x 3/32″ strip from a point aft of station 3 to the stem on each side. When this is done you need to mark three points along each side: at the transom, at station 3 and at the stem.

Then, mark a point just above the ½″ plank you just added at the stem.

At the transom mark a point on the side plank, ⅛″ below the top edge of the transom.

Clamp a batten between these points and strike a line.

While being careful not to cut into the side frames, cut through the hull along this line and discard the excess.

Frame 1 and 2.

Here's a view of the forward part of the boat and the stemliner.

Install the remainder of the side frames and a bottom frame ¾″ aft of frame #10. No side frame is required. Also install a side frame on the forward face of the mast step.

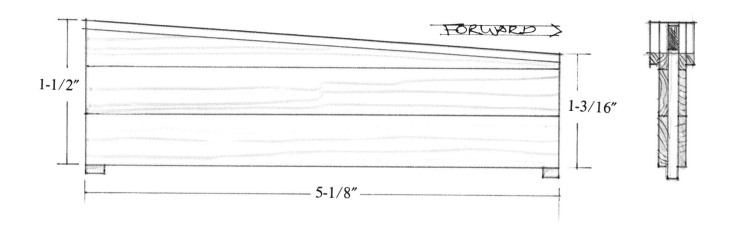

Details of the centerboard case.

Begin construction of the centerboard case by securing three ½" x 3/32" strips, 6" long, to a base. Strike lines at each end 5⅛" apart.

Strike a line from the top of the aft end to a point on the forward end that is 5/16" from the top. Cut.

Glue a piece of ¼" x 3/32" stock on the inside of each of these lines for end posts. Allow them to extend above and below the sides.

Cut the end posts off, leaving ⅛" below the bottom of the case.

Glue ½" strips on top of the end posts. Allow to dry. The square will help in the alignment.

The finished case. Add 3/32" x 3/32" trim at the top.

The centerboard case fits snugly between the station 3 bulkhead and the station 6 frame. Read the next few steps before you install it.

This is the frame forward of the mast step, which I mentioned earlier.

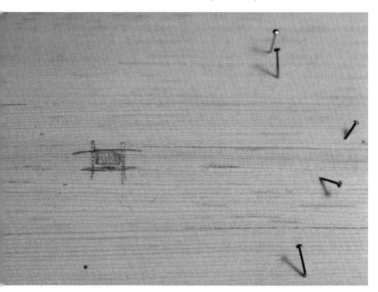

The end post penetrates the keelson.

The thwart rests on the #3 bulkhead and notches between the side frames. It also engages the centerboard case to form a rigid structure. The centerline mark will help later with the mast. The thwart is glued up from the same stock as the station 3 bulkhead. Fit it before the centerboard case is installed.

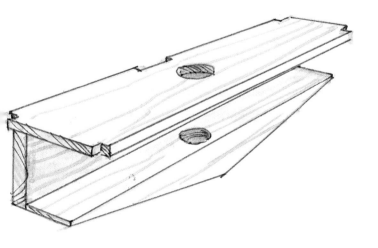

The mast head assembly

Between stations 3 and 6 are two equally spaced half-frames with corresponding side frames and small 3/32″ x 3/32″ x ½″ cleats where they fasten to the centerboard case.

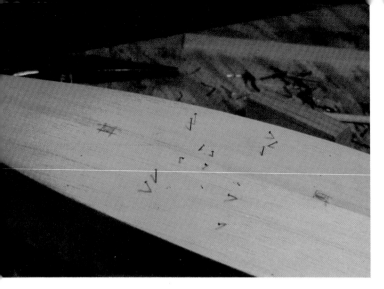

Pins may be necessary to pull the half frames into full contact with the bottom planks.

notch to fit the side frames.

A second thwart is fitted just aft of the centerboard case.

Glue and install. Brush away any excess glue.

Notch to fit the case and...

Put a cleat above the forward thwart.

Put a cleat under the aft thwart.

Use 3/32″ x 3/32″ stock for small cant frames under the deck supports.

Notch the sides forward of frame one for the forward deck.

Sand for a smooth surface.

Fit supports on the inside.

Glue ¾″ x 3/32″ stock transversely across the deck supports.

Just aft of frame 9 is an additional thwart. Use ¾″ x 3/32″ material. It notches into the frame. Glue a lip with some thin scrap to the aft edge to support the seat planks.

Measure a piece of ¾″ x 3/32″ stock.

Bevel a piece of ⅛″ x ¼″ stock.

Notch and trim to fit between the transom and the thwart behind frame 9.

Install about 1/16″ above the lower transom frame.

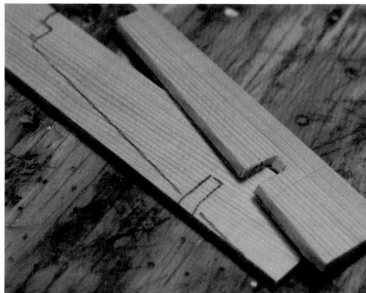

Use it to duplicate the opposite side.

Fill the space between the side pieces with ½″ x 3/32″ stock. Bevel the aft edges to fit the transom.

Use a piece of side frame stock to make the rudder post. Let it extend below the transom by 1″.

The finished seat.

Carve and sand the chunks at the bow to match the bottom profile and flow smoothly to the stem. Allow a ¼″ wide flat face at the center line for the shoe.

Fit a piece of ¼″ x 3/32″ stock between frames 3 and 4, port and starboard at the sheer.

Using ¾″ x ⅛″ stock as a guide, mark a point ¾″ above the bottom on the rudder post.

Then clamp the stock to the rudder post. This piece should contact the keelson at about station 6.

Mark for the cut at the rudder post.

Scribe with dividers set at ¾".

Glue and pin.

Cut and sand.

Trim off the rudder post.

Sand to a straight edge.

With a block under the foredeck, trim close to the sides.

Glue a piece of ⅛″ x ⅛″ stock from where it overlaps the centerboard case aft post to aft of the rudder post.

Sand the foredeck edges and the face of the stem liner.

When dry, trim and sand.

Glue the stem to the stem liner. Use a piece of 7/16″ x ½″ stock. Set aside to dry.

37

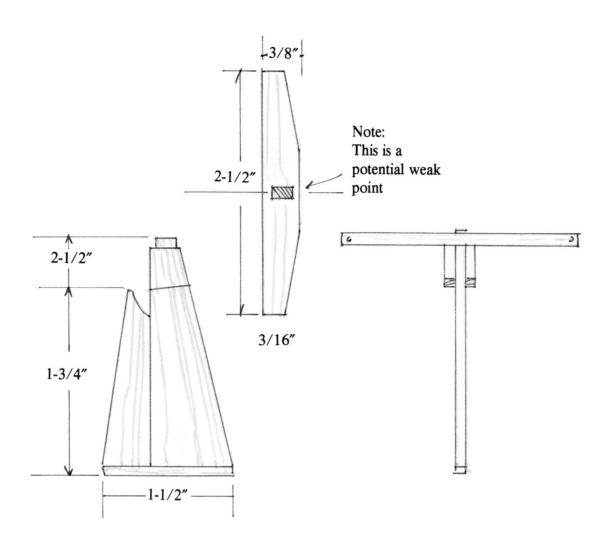

3/8″

Note:
This is a
potential weak
point

2-1/2″

3/16″

2-1/2″

1-3/4″

1-1/2″

The rudder assembly.

Lay out the rudder on side plank (1½″ x 3/32″) stock.

Cut it out.

Add cheeks and shoe piece. Set aside to dry.

Sand the best edge to a straight edge.

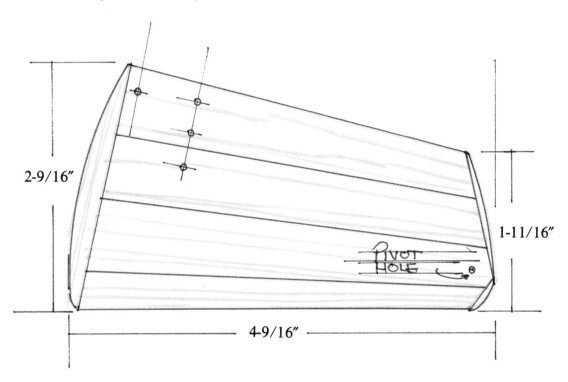

2-9/16"

1-11/16"

PIVOT HOLE

4-9/16"

Details of the centerboard.

To begin the centerboard, secure two pieces of side plank stock (about 6"
long) face to face. At one end come in about ⅜" on both sides and mark a
bevel. Cut with the saw.

Disassemble and glue butterfly-wise. Pin to a secure base until dry.

Glue ¼" x 3/32" stock between the transom and frame 10, and between frame 10 and frame 9 at the sheer. Use a sanding block to make the bevels. Glue securely.

Finished and installed cleats.

Using ¼" x 3/32" stock, carve small cleats. Look at the succeeding photos to understand the shape and the purpose before you begin.

When dry, carve away excess stock on the stem.

Install between frame 7 and 8 at the sheer, port and starboard.

Complete shaping the stem with the sanding block.

Here's where we are so far.

Remember our centerboard? Here it is, ready to shape.

Glue the shoe (¼″ x 3/32″ stock) on the area from just over the centerboard case post to and over the stem. Pin until dry.

Original dimensions not withstanding, it must fit inside the centerboard case, so double check.

Trim and, when dry, complete the final shaping with knife and sandpaper.

Use the template, but here I'm establishing the arc of the trailing edge.

41

The shape is correct and the cut lines are established.

The cut away pieces are used as templates for the final shape of the centerboard.

The cuts made. Reinforcing cross pieces will be the shape of the ends we just cut off. We use them as templates so don't lose them on the workshop floor.

The centerboard, finished and ready to install.

The reinforcing pieces attached.

Rub rail ready to glue to the hull at the sheer (these are 1/16″ x ⅛″ bass strips). These are glued on the side plank, with their top edge at the sheer.

A sanding block smooths the glue surface for the cap rail. It sits on top of the sheer and against the side frames.

Meanwhile, let's cut the centerboard slot. Drill out each end from the top with a 3/32″ bit.

Sanding in preparation for attaching the cap rail.

Cut out the wood between the holes. A knife with a guide is best.

The cap rail glued and pinned in place. Bevel the cap rail stock at the stem for a close fit.

Sand the opening.

Turn the hull back over and using the cap rail as a guide, trim off the side frames.

I drilled these holes before I actually installed the board. They're on a line about 1½″ forward of the trailing edge and about ⅜″ apart. The upper corner hole is ¼″ from the edge. I'll use a short length of a round toothpick for a pin.

Smooth any rough ends with a sanding block. Round the frame tops.

The rudder assembly has been trimmed and sanded and is ready for installation.

With the hull upright on a flat surface, insert the centerboard into its case as far as it'll go. Drive a nail through the case and the board about ½″ aft of the bulkhead and ¼″ above the keelson.

Lay out the yoke as per diagram. Cut out.

44

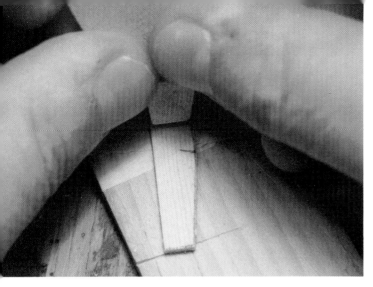

Use the boss on top of the rudder to impress a mark the size of the hole in the yoke.

Mark and drill holes for rudder hinges in the rudder post.

Ready to assemble.

Mark corresponding but slightly offset holes in the rudder. The rudder side of the hinge rests on top of the rudder post side.

Glued and sanded.

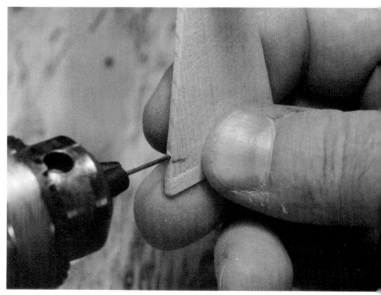

Drill the rudder.

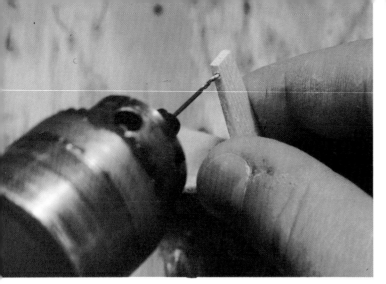

Drill the rope holes at the ends of the yoke at the same time.

Glue in place with cynoacrylic glue (medium speed).

Make the eyes from 22 gauge galvanized steel wire.

Drill a hole near the top of the rudder post.

Clip off at about ¼".

Cut a groove with the knife.

Bend a hook in the end of a 1/32″ brass rod.

Clip off the bottom.

Thread the rod down through the eyes.

Drill fair leads in the rails at the stern. There are four, equally spaced. Use a 1/16″ bit. Drill four holes in the rails between frames 3 and 4.

Glue the hook into the groove.

Chamfer the edges of the holes with a larger drill bit. Drill and chamfer a small hole in the fore deck just aft of the stemliner (for the deck line).

Drill the hole in the thwart above the mast step, with a ⅜″ bit. I do this slowly by hand to prevent splintering.

Now that it's drilled, sand smooth. Find the center and drill a shallow ¼″ hole in the mast step.

Our boat so far.

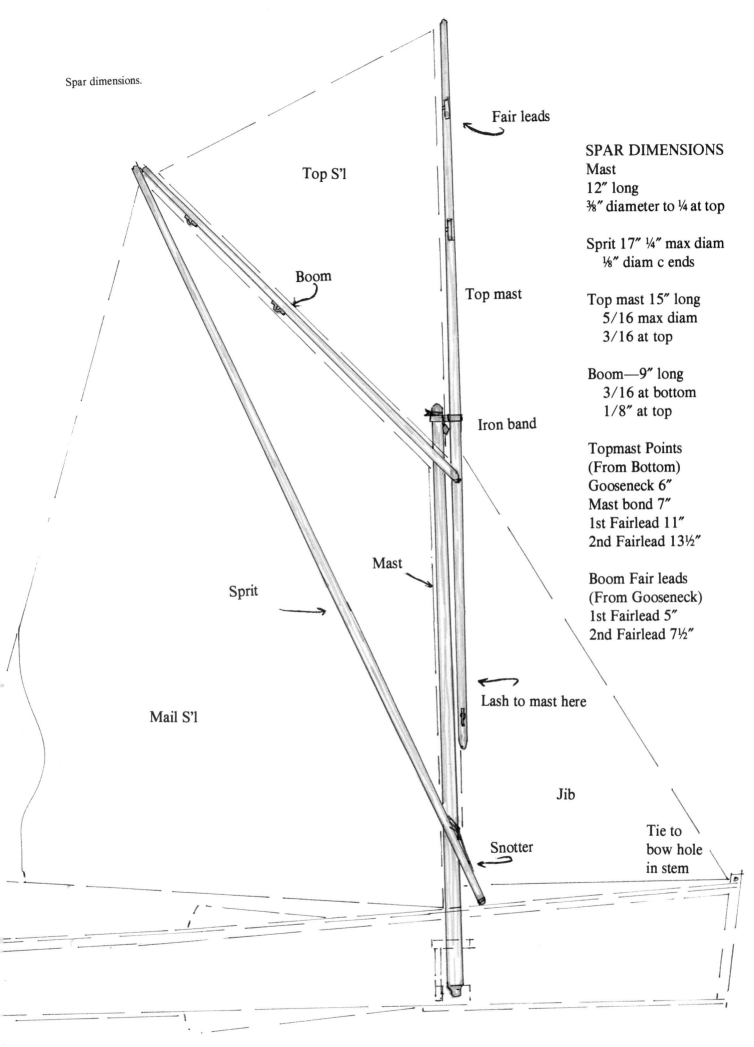

Spar dimensions.

Fair leads

Top S'l

Boom

Top mast

Iron band

Mast

Sprit

Mail S'l

Lash to mast here

Jib

Snotter

Tie to
bow hole
in stem

SPAR DIMENSIONS
Mast
12″ long
⅜″ diameter to ¼ at top

Sprit 17″ ¼″ max diam
⅛″ diam c ends

Top mast 15″ long
5/16 max diam
3/16 at top

Boom—9″ long
3/16 at bottom
1/8″ at top

Topmast Points
(From Bottom)
Gooseneck 6″
Mast bond 7″
1st Fairlead 11″
2nd Fairlead 13½″

Boom Fair leads
(From Gooseneck)
1st Fairlead 5″
2nd Fairlead 7½″

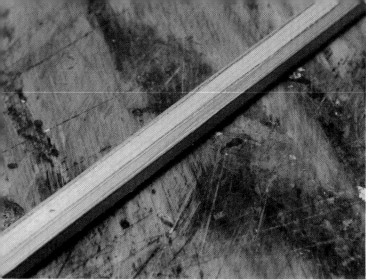

Shaping spars from square stock is done by just planing it to eight-sided piece, then rounding it with sandpaper. These lines are just guides. This is ½″ stock for the mast.

Finish sanding with fine sandpaper.

Once the piece is octagonal, plane the taper.

Trim the end and measure 12″ to the bottom.

Round off with the sanding block.

Carve a little taper and a ¼″ plus boss at the base.

Dry fit before finishing.

Sand a surface for the fairleads.

Drill 1/16″ hole, ¼″ below the top for the halyard hole.

Glue in place 3/32″ x 3/32″ stock ⅜″ long.

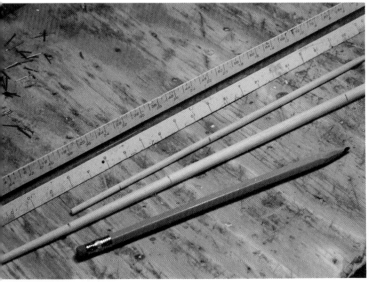

Plane and sand the topsail mast assembly spars in the same way as the mast. Measure and mark the position of the topsail brail fairleads and the gooseneck joint.

Carve to shape when dry.

51

Stabilize with penetrating super glue.

Make one eye.

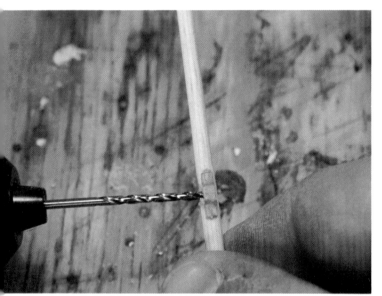

Drill with 1/16″ drill bit.

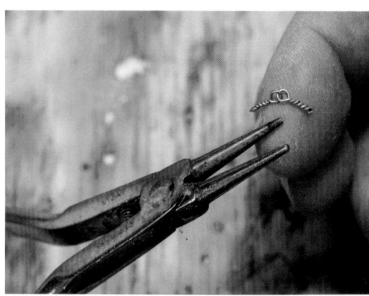

Articulate it with the second eye.

Finished fairlead. Sand lightly.

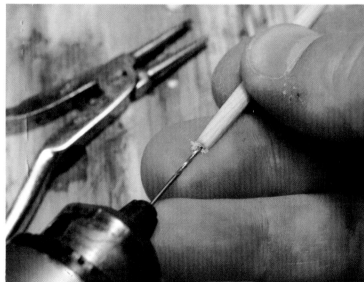

Drill the end of the topsail boom and the topsail mast. Insert and glue the eye assembly. Don't forget the sprit. Stain all the spars.

Painting and Sailmaking

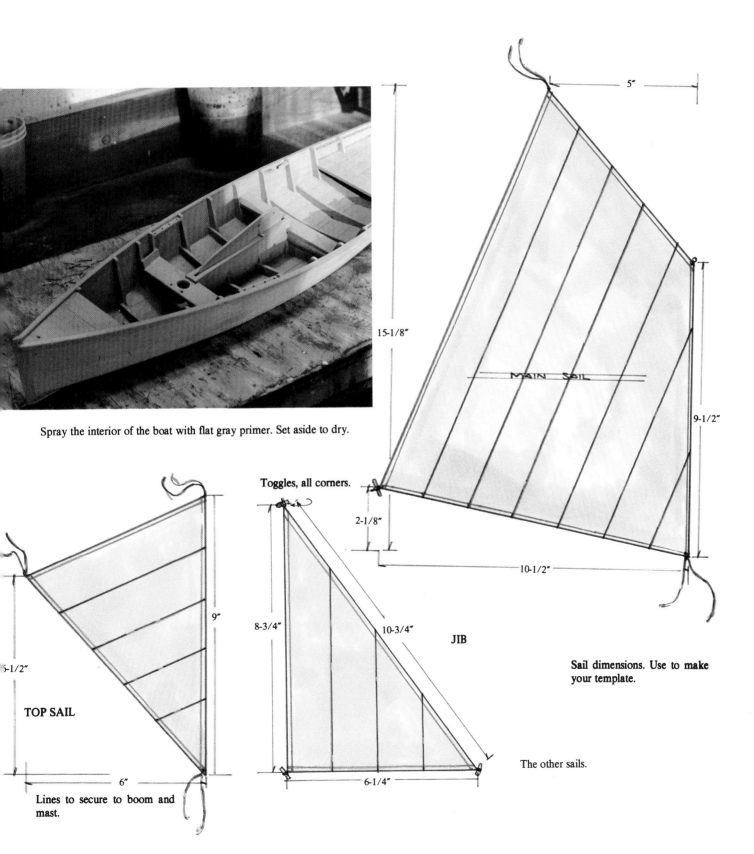

Spray the interior of the boat with flat gray primer. Set aside to dry.

5″

15-1/8″

MAIN SAIL

9-1/2″

Toggles, all corners.

2-1/8″

10-1/2″

9″

8-3/4″

10-3/4″

JIB

5-1/2″

TOP SAIL

Sail dimensions. Use to make your template.

6″

6-1/4″

The other sails.

Lines to secure to boom and mast.

Make your sail templates while you wait for the boat and the spars to dry. Make a pattern for your sails out of any fairly stiff material, i.e., cardboard.

Allow to dry thoroughly.

Paint the hull flat white (I use Latex ceiling paint).

On a large flat work surface stabilize the boat level with wedges. Block it with a very slight bow-up attitude.

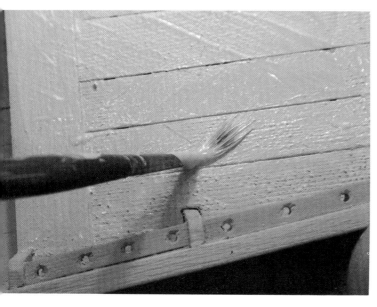

Paint the decks, thwarts, cup rails, and rudder yoke light green.

Lay down a few scraps of plywood beside the boat even with the desired water line. Lay a pencil flat on the plywood, and swing it back and forth to lightly scribe a line. Move the plywood stock around the boat to complete the water line.

Tape the lines and rub to thoroughly press the tape down.

Remove the tape.

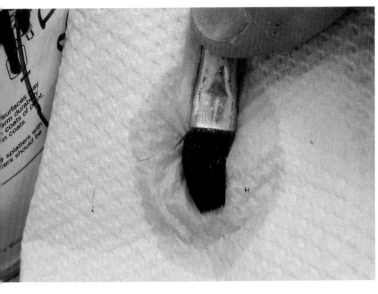

Use a paper towel to draw out any possible water in the ferrule of the brush.

After it's thoroughly dried carefully hand sand the exposed corners and surfaces of the hull.

Paint the bottom reddish brown. I use exterior latex house paint. The color is redwood with a little black added.

Don't overdo it, but do develop the worn-paint look, characteristic of most working craft.

Use fine sandpaper on the bottom in order to bring out the grain.

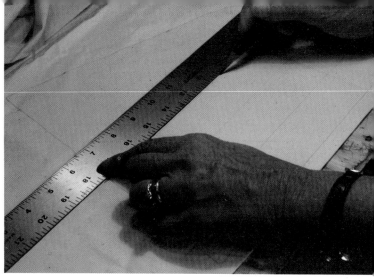

Use a ruler or straight edge to connect the dots; you now have your seam lines.

Your boat now begins to look realistic.

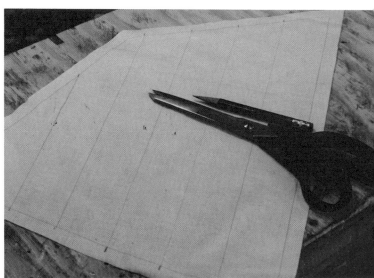

Mark a line about ½″ out from the edges of the sail. Cut on this line.

Lay the sail pattern on the unbleached muslin, the longest edge of the sail parallel to the selvages, on the straight grain of the fabric. Trace the outline lightly with a pencil and also mark the seam lines by making a dot on two edges of the sail.

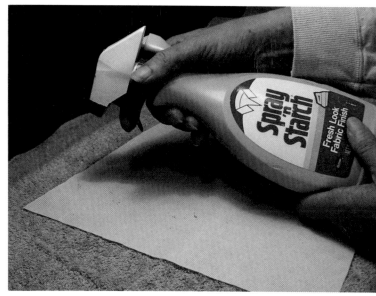

Spray with water or starch. This makes the edges of the sails easier to turn under.

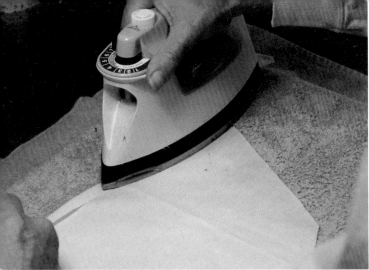

Fold over the edges of the sails and press with an iron.

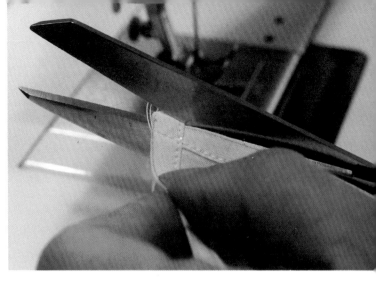

Trim the thread and any excess material on the sail corners.

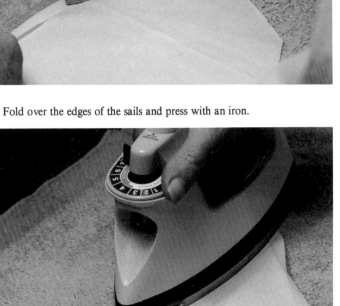

Turn under the folded edges and press. You now have finished edges.

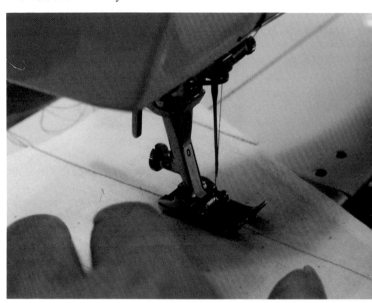

Sew with brown thread along the seam lines. Trim.

Sew along the folded edges with the white thread. When starting to sew on one of the corners of the sails, it helps to hold the bobbin and top thread and apply a little tension; this helps to prevent the sail corner from going down into the throat plate of the sewing machine.

The finished sail is now ready for staining.

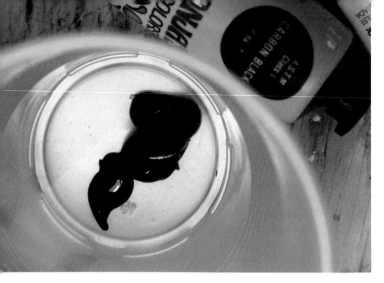

I mix burnt umber acrylic paint with a little black, add a little water and mix very thoroughly. Don't allow any color particles to remain.

Form the band around the topsail mast and solder.

This is the desired color. Thoroughly soak the sails in warm water, then dip them in the stain. Finally, rinse them again in warm water until the color is a medium tan, then throw them into the dryer.

Crimp around the main mast and solder.

Install the main mast.

Use a pin to form a small eye at the base of the mast.

Pin and glue a cleat at the end of the topsail mast. The brails for opening and closing the topsail both tie here, run up to their respective starboard fairleads out to the boom, and back to the topsail mast where they tie off at their respective port fairleads.

This piece of sheet metal came from a can lid, flattened with a hammer.

Glue and pin cleats on either side of the main mast at the base.

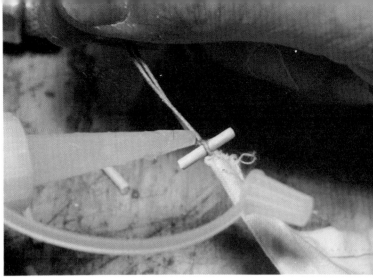

Tie and glue toggles to all points on the jib and where the sheet line attaches to the mainsail.

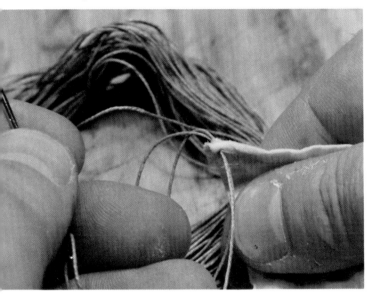

Use rigging line to sew lines into all the sail corners except on the halyard point on the mainsail.

Make a wire eye at the halyard point on the mainsail.

Round toothpicks cut about ⅜" long make good toggles.

Tie a block to the top of the mast for the jib.

Super glue hardens the ends of your lines and makes it easier to thread the blocks and fairleads.

The sheet line from the jib threads through the port and starboard fairleads and ties off at the forward port and starboard cleats. Use a clove hitch.

Begin your lines at the cleats. A credible amount of line adds realism.

Lace the mainsail to the mast, starting at the halyard. Lace back and forth, not around. Tie off at the bottom. The main sheet line and the topsail line run through the aft fairlead...

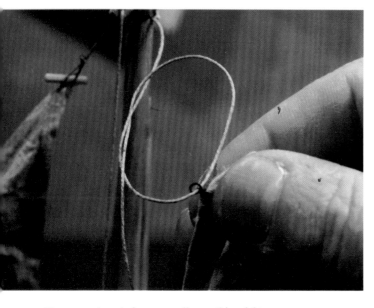

Form your knot before you pull everything tight.

and tie off at the midships cleats.

The rudder yoke line is about 30 inches long and is knotted and glued through the yoke.

There's enough mass to the centerboard structure to allow 3/32″ brass rods for mounting on a driftwood base. Drill and glue.

A lanyard keeps the center board peg from getting lost.

Our model is ready for painting.

The "snotter" ties around the mainmast and holds the sprit. The mainsail peak ties to the other end of the sprit. The snotter is a little over 2″ long with a ⅛″ eye at one end.

I make a black wash out of a diluted solution of drafting ink. This will give you an idea of the intensity.

I sprayed the entire boat with clean water. Now I'm covering it with black wash.

This is the rust wash made from yellow-orange azo, burnt sienna, and burnt umber, thinned with water.

Wash away the excess black.

I apply the rust wash sparingly and only where it would logically stain the hull inside and out.